This Book Belongs to:

_____

Louis Weber, C.E.O.
Publications International, Ltd.
7373 North Cicero Avenue
Lincolnwood, Illinois 60646

Manufactured in USA.

ISBN: 0-7853-0404-5

# THE HOKEY-POKEY

### ILLUSTRATED BY
### LINDA DOCKEY GRAVES

Publications International, Ltd.

You put your right foot in,
    You put your right foot out;

You put your right foot in,
    And you shake it all about.

You do the Hokey-Pokey,
    And you turn yourself around.

That's what it's all about!

You put your left foot in,
   You put your left foot out;
You put your left foot in,
   And you shake it all about.
You do the Hokey-Pokey,
   And you turn yourself around.
That's what it's all about!

You put your right hand in,
  You put your right hand out;
You put your right hand in,
  And you shake it all about.
You do the Hokey-Pokey,
  And you turn yourself around.
That's what it's all about!

You put your left hand in,
   You put your left hand out;
You put your left hand in,
   And you shake it all about.
You do the Hokey-Pokey,
   And you turn yourself around.
That's what it's all about!

You put your right side in,
    You put your right side out;
You put your right side in,
    And you shake it all about.
You do the Hokey-Pokey,
    And you turn yourself around.
That's what it's all about!

You put your left side in,
    You put your left side out;
You put your left side in,
    And you shake it all about.
You do the Hokey-Pokey,
    And you turn yourself around.
That's what it's all about!

You put your nose in,
    You put your nose out;

You put your nose in,
    And you shake it all about.

You do the Hokey-Pokey,
    And you turn yourself around.

That's what it's all about!

You put your tail in,
　　You put your tail out;
You put your tail in,
　　And you shake it all about.
You do the Hokey-Pokey,
　　And you turn yourself around.
That's what it's all about!

You put your head in,
    You put your head out;
You put your head in,
    And you shake it all about.
You do the Hokey-Pokey,
    And you turn yourself around.
That's what it's all about!

You put your whole self in,
  You put your whole self out;
You put your whole self in,
  And you shake it all about.
You do the Hokey-Pokey,
  And you turn yourself around.
That's what it's all about!